Text
Hugh Pearman

Photography
Alan Williams
Chris Gascoigne

Blueprint
Extra

# 10

The Ark
London

Architect
Ralph Erskine

To find a new city building that appears to have a sense of fun and adventure is rare enough. To find such a building serving as a landmark at a key urban gateway is rarer still. And to discover that the building is one of the very few works in Britain by one of the great names of modern architecture makes it remarkable. But such is our ability to absorb the extraordinary, that The Ark by Ralph Erskine, situated in Hammersmith on the western fringe of central London, is already an accepted, if inevitably sometimes controversial, part of the urban landscape.

When first mooted, it seemed – to conservative British tastes – a Quixotic kind of object, a perhaps unnecessarily romantic response to a difficult setting. Pragmatists assured themselves and others that it would never be built as designed, that it would not lend itself to fast-track construction techniques, and would inevitably be reduced by the usual process of economic and aesthetic attrition to a shadow of its intended glory. But then it was built, and here it is, pretty much as Erskine intended: a totemic structure outside, a democratically-organised working environment inside. It is safe to say that it does not look the part of the standard British developer's office block of its period.

To understand the building, it is necessary to understand something about the man who designed it. Ralph Erskine was born in England in

1914 and was educated on humane Quaker principles at Saffron Walden, in Essex. A believer in a progressive and just society, he left England for Sweden in 1939, completed his studies at the Stockholm Art Academy, and set up his office first in "The Box", his own home in the country, and then in Drottningholm in 1946. He has practised ever since from what, to other Europeans, seems like a peculiarly remote location, adding to the Erskine mystique. Here was an Englishman who chose to build in the snowbound north, opting for a natural environment even harsher than his own.

Moreover Erskine, who during the 1950s affiliated himself to the precepts of the radical Team X group, which included such other luminaries as Aldo van Eyck, Giancarlo de Carlo and Alison and Peter Smithson, was from the first a strong believer in individual, rather than formulaic international-modern, architecture. As such Team X, which emerged from and effectively destroyed the increasingly directionless modern architecture talking-shop CIAM, represented a new departure in architecture. And yet Erskine had put in more than a decade of highly individualist architecture, helping to develop a new strand of Scandinavian modernism, before Team X emerged.

Erskine's buildings respond directly to their context and to

the needs of their users. From the early days designing what would now be called "organic" snow-covered structures in the far north, he graduated to city housing schemes and, immediately prior to The Ark, a major office building in Gothenburg which displays some of the thinking of the later building. But his has always been an eclectic canon of projects. Few other architects could include Greenland and northern Canada on their list of sites, but on the other hand this midnight-sun voyaging, a calculatedly alternative route to that taken by his colleagues in the European or American mainstreams, carried the risk that Erskine's developing strengths might be overlooked or simply seen as being of merely parochial interest. The Team X link, then, helped bring Erskine to early critical attention.

When he returned to Britain in the late 1960s, first to build an accommodation wing at Clare Hall in Cambridge and some housing in in Newmarket and in Milton Keynes, and then to north-east England to design what became known as the Byker Wall, accolades were to flow from his country of birth. Although some design carry-over is apparent from the relatively miniscule Cambridge scheme and earlier projects in Sweden, he more or less invented what was later to be hijacked and diluted by others under the banner of "community architecture". Byker was a

The Ark is the antithesis of the conventional speculative office building with standard spaces and rectangular floor plates. Here, each floor provides a different experience. The scale and variety of form enhances the vertiginous quality of the atria.
Opposite page: looking up to the timber clad ceiling in one of The Ark's circular atria.

Top: At the Byker development in Newcastle-upon-Tyne, Erskine involved the local community in the design process to create an environment which avoided the troubles that have plagued so many large-scale public housing projects.
Above: The Lilla Bommen building in Gothenberg displays some of the thinking to be found in The Ark.

Herman Hertzberg's 1961 Centraal Beheer office building in Apeldoorn, left, was a pioneering example of the concept of office-as-community. Erskine took his Ark clients to see the building early in the design process.

community living in run-down housing when Erskine arrived. By the time he left, over ten years later, the slums had gone but the 9,500-strong community remained, rehoused in a development of astonishing richness and complexity and showing several touches of Erskinian whimsy. The "wall" element was only part of it – an embracing and sheltering form for much else, including the single family dwellings that most people asked for, and got. And yet the local community had played a leading part in the decision-making process as the vast scheme developed.

Its success (despite some teething troubles) can be judged by the fact that Byker is not much talked about these days. Unlike other megaschemes of its period, it appears not to have gone significantly wrong and is, conversely, particularly liked. Lushly landscaped, it survived not only the community architecture bandwagon, but even the voguish wave of stained-timber detailing it inspired in Britain throughout the 1980s.

Byker may have made Erskine a hero to a generation of British architects, but it was scarcely a preparation for The Ark except perhaps in the notion of a strong form acting as a shelter for its inhabitants against traffic. When the invitation came from the Swedish developers, Åke Larson and Pronator, to design an office block in Hammersmith, conditions were

The Ark is an urban building that delights in its juxtaposition with a filling station, motorway and railway line. Since it has no context to defer to, it has instead developed its own.

entirely different. Not only was the site unpromising, being between one of the more heavily-used traffic intersections in London and Underground tracks in a cutting, but the final users of the building were not known. His clients, however, who intended moving into some of the space themselves, were both familiar with and approving of the Scandinavian "democratic office" principles that Erskine espoused. It is significant that he took his clients early on to see Herman Herzberger's Centraal Beheer insurance building in Apeldoorn in the Netherlands, designed in 1961 and a pioneering example of the office-as-community, where the interior is the main concern. Equally important is that Erskine's clients were prepared to let him do things his way.

Erskine maintains a tiny office, and works in collaboration with other trusted architects in order to retain personal design freedom at the sharp end of things. In the case of what was to become The Ark, his initial response was entirely typical: he did not want to do the job. The site was too inhuman, there was little by way of a sympathetic context to respond to. A feasibility study had been carried out on the site – previously a car pound – by the London architects Rock Townsend, and this had, for the purposes of establishing the site's viability, suggested a vertical-walled scheme to face up to the drear elevation of a Novotel across the road. His

collaborations with Rock Townsend and later with Lennart Bergström's office in Stockholm were to prove crucial to the building of The Ark. But at this stage the possibilities indicated for the site seemed to confirm Erskine's misgivings, and he relinquished the commission.

It's easy to understand this initial feeling of recoil. Britain, in the late 1980s, was in the grip of extreme architectural conservatism. Office complexes such as the nearby, hamfistedly post-modern, Hammersmith Broadway development, which was about to start on site, appeared to be the preference of many. Few architects at his age, and with no previous London building to their name, would want to plunge into what was physically as well as bureaucratically a maelstrom.

But typically, when he started thinking about Åke Larson and Pronator's ideals about creating a more humane work environment, Erskine changed his mind. He came back to the project not only because of the faith placed in him by Åke Larson, but also because he had worked out how he could cope with the situation. If the building had no context to respond to, then it would simply have to create its own context. Inside would be a complete working and social environment, a virtually self-sufficient community. Perhaps a sneaking desire to build finally in London, where he had studied at Regent Street Polytechnic

in the late 1930s, also played a part.

The challenge was the interior environment, and the exterior would follow. The form of The Ark, therefore, did not spring fully-formed from Erskine's fertile imagination. This was to be a fast-track project, a building method which, although it allows design work to overlap with building, means that a clear concept must be agreed before work begins.

Erskine chewed over the scheme in its early stages with his old collaborator from Byker Wall days, Vernon Gracie. What emerged from their design deliberations was this: a building with a rounded triangular plan that flares upwards from its base, to maximise the volume of the community atrium and minimise the dark north elevation facing the Novotel. Conversely it allows a perimeter access road and a certain amount of landscaping on the very tight site (made tighter by the fact that some "planning gain", in the form of a low adjacent building for the local council, also had to be accommodated). Rising to nine floors on its defensive northern flank, it was to step away in plant-festooned terraces to five floors on the southern side where, although a busy railway cutting for London Underground trains intervened, the context is streets of brick-built late nineteenth-century terraced houses.

Later this was to prove a problem when local residents claimed that the building reflected and amplified the noise of the railway. Erskine

Erskine's early sketches show how his response to the local environment and climatic aspects determined the form of the building.

investigated the situation and remarks: "The problems of reflected noise to neighbours across the railway are unfortunately considerable. The building protects against traffic noise but, as always with urban routes, reflects the adjacent railway noise.

"Though the noise level is measured and found to be below the official 'nuisance' level, it has a most aggressive character due to the deplorable worn state of the rails. Requests to London Underground that it should at least maintain, and preferably weld, the rails – the reasonable solution to the problem – has so far not led to any action. The alternative, which is to cover over the tracks with non-residential functions, has attracted no finance to date. The only other solution would have been minimum development, but it is more likely that this central site would have remained a desolate car pound or become an undesirable park."

The sleek sides of the building – originally intended to be white – were to rise to an intriguingly busy roofscape, a dramatic gesture generated by colliding geometries. This roof was to be a shallow vault roughly cut to size and perched on top like a peaked cap at a jaunty angle. Not satisfied merely with that, Erskine proposed to split the roof down the centre with a glazed slot, puncture it with twin glazed domes that would cling like limpets to the slope, and send a lift shaft shooting

The Lilla Huset or Little House, left, was built for the local council, as "planning gain" for the development. Below: The Ark is an important landmark in this part of West London, eclipsing the low-grade post-modernism of the adjacent development at Hammersmith Broadway.

up through it to culminate in an observation gallery. The roofslot was to continue down the front of the building, aligned with the tower of nearby St Paul's parish church – an uncharacteristically staid exercise by those Victorian mavericks Roumieu, Gough and Seddon.

Local consultation revealed a degree of concern about a building that looked too much like a landed spaceship, and at an early stage Erskine proposed a different palette of materials. The roof and the spandrel panels for the sloping sides would be copper, at first appearing brown and then oxidising gradually to bright green. The glazing would be tinted a brown that, Erskine insisted, should be exactly that of the Newcastle Brown Ale he was familiar with from Byker days. Red brick would clad the stumpy pillars which act visually as the building's "feet", and much use of light wood would be made inside.

Erskine and Gracie dwelt in particular on the hierarchy of spaces in the interior, which though "flexible" in developer's jargon, were to be quite unlike the standard Burolandschaft approach of wide open-plan prairies. The staggered floors – stepping back from the central atrium in a manner reflected faithfully in the outer form of the building – were modified with a sequence of subsidiary spaces that were intended to give the occupants of each level a sense of place. The concept was agreed: in The Ark, you

The early proposal for white cladding, shown in this model, gave way to copper whose brown finish will gradually oxidise to green.

would know where you were and where you were going. The interior would be its own map. External terraces would be intimate and friendly, and face the sun.

With all this done, there remained the little matter of making the building buildable, and here Rock Townsend, and later Lennart Bergström, came back into the picture. Erskine and Gracie had not designed a building that lent itself to easy construction.

Rock Townsend had pioneered the concept of the democratic workspace in Britain, and were fully in accord with the Erskine philosophy, as were Bergström: more difficult was making it all fit together. That meant, above all, rationalising the geometries involved and arriving at the most suitable structure. For a year and four months, between July 1988 and November 1989, Rock Townsend, under partner Alastair Hay, and the English and Swedish engineers (with the latter led by Bengt Leidner) exchanged sketches by fax with Erskine in Sweden, with the two sides meeting up every few weeks to discuss progress.

The Ark went through considerable development in this period, and more was to occur as it was being built. One difficulty was finding a way to clad a building if a true double-curved external wall was desired. Mullions of glass must widen as they progress up the building. It was not impossible, but

standard curtain-walling systems just could not handle it at a reasonable cost. The solution was soon agreed upon, to design the exterior as a sequence of flat conic segments to handle the taper, with the top two levels on the high side treated vertically. The brown solar shading was confined to a sandwich of separate glazing panels on each level, with a band of brown glass above and below a clear central panel. Such modifications, to adjust the building both to cost and human experience, were equally important for Erskine and the clients.

Erskine, according to reports, adopted the attitude of the pragmatist rather than the prima-donna during the working-drawings stage, trading off one element of the building against another. Furthermore, his real concern throughout was with the way the interior looked and worked rather than with the cladding details. These he discussed with the manufacturers in England and twice in visits to firms in Italy.

It was around this time that the building started to be dubbed "The Ark". Erskine, true to his Modernist principles, had not designed a hull-shape for the sake of it even if, like Noah, he had designed his building as a self-contained community to float serenely above the surrounding chaos. Some like to think that the name "Ark" stems from a British mispronunciation of the first name of the Swedish construction and

The full drama of the atrium does not become apparent until the visitor starts to move up the building – unlike many office atria where the space is immediately apparent. Erskine was keen to get away from the boring atrium floor, conventionally decorated with potted trees and waterfalls.

Ralph Erskine's sketches showing section through the facade and the central atrium feature.

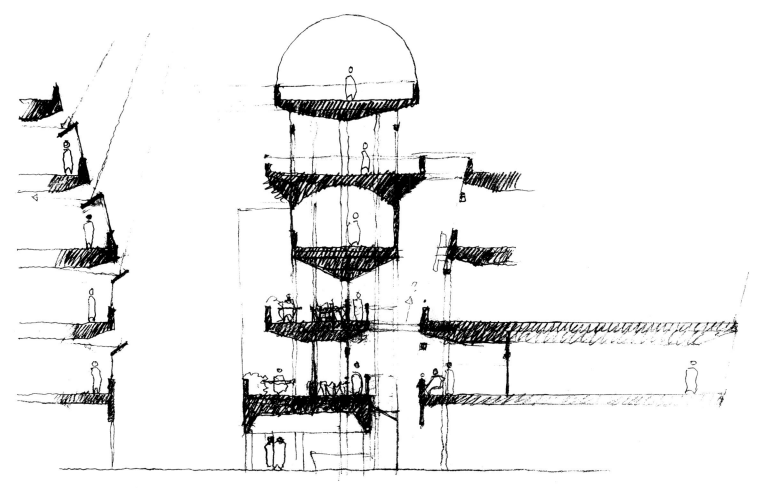

project managers, Åke Larson. But the truth was that, in a clear case of morphic resonance, virtually every commentator who saw the original drawings immediately used this nautical metaphor, and many passers by, seeing the finished product, have done likewise. Had it been finished in lighter-coloured materials it might just as well have been called the "Egg", given Erskine's concept of a hard outer shell protecting a soft interior. Other critics have recognised The Ark as a womb-like building.

The end result, with its eclectic mix of materials, could be read as British or Swedish depending on your perception of Erskine. In his adopted Sweden, his work is sometimes seen as being very English in outlook. In England it is recognised that he has captured the Scandinavian aesthetic more successfully than any of his contemporaries back home. Remember, too, that it was the progressive social attitudes of Sweden that attracted Erskine to that country in the first place. The Ark was being designed at the height of the entrepreneurial 1980s – the Thatcher era – in Britain. Erskine summed it up at the time thus: "If I go into a pub I feel very English. I suspect that if I met Maggie Thatcher, I would feel very Swedish."

The pub, that time-proven concept of a democratic meeting-place, soon found its way into

The eyrie at the top of the building, left, provides 180-degree views of the surrounding area. The sensation of exposure that it creates is in direct contrast to the Scandinavian cosiness of "Ralph's pub", below, that is on the ground floor.

The Ark. Erskine's conical atrium, reflected in the external shape of the building and rising to the curved underbelly of the roof, was anyway discernibly different in character from the standard developer's fare – an arena rather than a glorified lightwell. Even so it could have been an intimidating space. Erskine with some justification regarded most atrium floors as boring in the extreme – no matter how many trees and waterfalls the developers and their architects installed. In a relatively late design decision, he proposed building a village on the atrium floor. This was to be an almost mediaeval settlement of tall buildings and narrow alleys, and would incorporate – naturally enough – a pub, soon to be known as Ralph's pub.

A model was made of the atrium-floor buildings and, seen in isolation, the complex could function perfectly well as a piece of architecture in its own right. But the main purpose of this seemingly bizarre decision was to bring people nearer to one another and at the same time to express this nearness by modifying the visual impact of The Ark's spectacular interior. Instead of emerging from the compressed space of the entrance lobby into a sudden great space, the secrets of what lay above were to be more gradually revealed.

As if to prove that one of the principal problems with the English planning system is that architects

Erskine's sketch of the interior of the atrium with a pub at ground level has an urban feel to it – it has the atmosphere of a busy square rather than a speculative office block.

too often design what they think planners will most easily approve, The Ark sailed through the planning process virtually unscathed, supported both by the local planners and by the Government-funded architectural watchdog, the Royal Fine Art Commission. Åke Larson had taken the somewhat risky step of indicating that, if the scheme was refused planning permission, he would not appeal and go through the agonies of negotiating and redesigning. The gamble paid off: planning permission was granted on 19 September 1989 and the developers moved their diggers on to the site the same day.

Erskine's working method is to stay as much as possible at his base in Drottningholm. But the international design-by-fax process was deemed insufficient for detail design, and in November 1989, The Ark design team was moved to Stockholm, to the offices of Erskine's long-time collaborators Lennart Bergström Architects who (in a further testament to Erskine's single-minded way of doing things) own his office and employ all his staff leaving him free to design. Two Rock Townsend design staff went and joined the fifteen-strong Bergström team in Stockholm which was led by Bosse Svensson and Lars Wilson. Their colleagues back home pored over British Building Regulations and worked on the "planning gain" building for the council alongside, known as the

The snorkel-like protruberances, glazed dome and variegated profile reinforce the building's nautical title. The top-level meeting room, right, is reached via a dramatic ride through the building in a glazed lift.

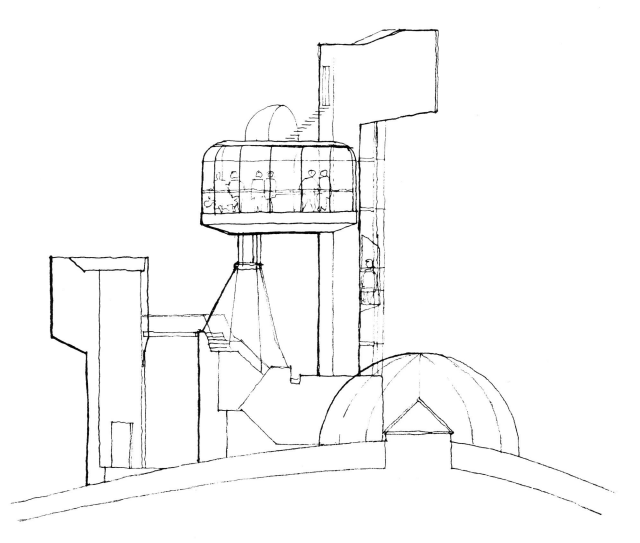

The drawings of the roofscape suggest a series of separate exercises creating a mini-village at the top of the building. The built version was simpler and more striking.

The view across
the rail tracks from
the south gives a
clear explanation of
the organisation
of the building, with
the sweeping copper
roof supported on
brick cores which
punch through
the sloping skin.

Lilla Huset, or Little House.

The Swedish way of working – in which the architect is employed directly by the client, as are all the other consultants and sub-contractors – in theory meant a diminished role for Erskine, although he was in charge of the other disciplines in practice, if not legally. In the interests of speed and cost, some detailing was left to the contractors, which partly explains the over-engineered nature of the exposed truss supporting the atrium roof beneath its light-slot, despite the fact that all such details were checked and adjusted by Erskine and the team.

But this is not a high-tech building, in the stylistic sense whereby design engineers of repute are needed to create the necessary purity of structure. To this extent the tight detailing of the exterior curtain wall belies the more usual Scandinavian approach in the interior, which is a much looser-fit affair. The real cleverness comes in places which many might not even consider, such as the way the "legs" of the building, which are clad in rough brick of the kind usually intended to be rendered, penetrate the smooth skin and continue in the interior. The junctions at these points were some of the trickiest details that Rock Townsend had to deal with. As one of the job architects, Gordon Swapp, puts it: "Ralph did the rough sketch and then stood back: from then on, it

was in the hands of the executive architects to carry the baton."

Erskine was not able, however, to persuade his clients to continue the rough brick inside on the stair towers, though he managed to make it re-appear to the side of the atrium on the southerly terraces.

A legend developed around Erskine as the job progressed. It was said that he would never turn up on site at scheduled meetings, preferring rather to arrive unannounced. His disarming way of accepting alterations in one place was, it was soon realised, also his method of achieving something he deemed more important elsewhere. This mattered because Erskine's own method of working was to keep modifying his designs as work progressed. As various parts of the building reached their design freeze-point, he would turn his attention to another area, but check back at suitable intervals.

As built, The Ark is a one-off for London. Swedish developers had over-extended themselves badly overseas in the late 1980s due to the relaxing of exchange controls and learned some hard financial lessons as a result. Erskine's subsequent designs for stations on the Crossrail rapid rail link under London dealt with rather different concerns. And unlike precision-engineered technology-driven buildings, where what you see on completion is what you get for as long as the gaskets last, The Ark is a building designed

to weather and change. It developed at first in its external appearance, as the initially glittering copper roof and inclined spandrel panels oxidised, unevenly as planned, to green, affecting the patina of the brickwork in the process. And its internal character, though dramatic when empty, was always intended to take on the character of the eventual occupants of the building.

It is in its interior, of course, that the most impressive architecture of The Ark is to be found. The great defect of conventional spec buildings is that the architecture is merely a skin: inside you find the same generally rectangular office floorplates and suspended ceiling everywhere. The Ark offers an internal structure that can be travelled through and experienced in a number of ways – vertically and horizontally.

The big sensation is to rise through the buildings of the atrium floor on the lift that shoots towards and through the roof to arrive in the crow's-nest observation gallery on top, which is not a gimmick, but a usefully-sized room for small meetings. Below, that great curving roof, its underbelly lined with rough timber slats, effortlessly slides from the inside to the outside, setting the tone for the whole building.

To British eyes, it is an unusual mixture of the rough and the ready. Everywhere there are spaces that exist solely in order to be spaces:

there is the circular planted floor of the rotunda at one end of the atrium, for example, which matches the circular lobby area but has a completely different feel; or the numerous platforms and terraces, both inside and out, designed for informal meetings of whatever kind. There is a hierarchy of spaces built-in even before any tenant starts to mark out areas for particular individuals or groups of individuals. It might go against the idea of Burolandschaft as the ultimate democratic space, but then the dogmatic open-plan approach always found itself subverted, either by the bosses or by the workforce, in order to create private places anyway.

In the end, the true test of The Ark will be not so much the way it adapts to its users, but the way its users will adapt to it, and find their ways changed as a result. It is hoped that it will be occupied by several medium-sized firms who understand, interact with and thrive in an inspiring work community and change it from an "interesting building" to an environment which influences office planning internationally.

Meanwhile, Erskine's alchemical reputation is duly enhanced as, once again, he has designed a place of pilgrimage only to vanish to his Swedish retreat, leaving London all the richer for this characterful and characteristic contribution to the city.

A vertical strip of glazing cuts through the western façade of the building, marking the entrance to the offices. It carves into the protective nature of the cladding revealing the soft centre – see pages 18 to 21 overleaf.

The lattice dome sits above the series of levels created within the atrium space. These were added at a fairly late stage in the design process in order to reduce the intimidating nature of a single open volume. See also pages 24 to 27 overleaf.

As is the convention, the atrium is adorned with glazed wall climbers – the big sensation is to rise through the building from the atrium floor, into the atrium space and then to shoot through the roof to arrive at the crow's nest meeting-room on top.

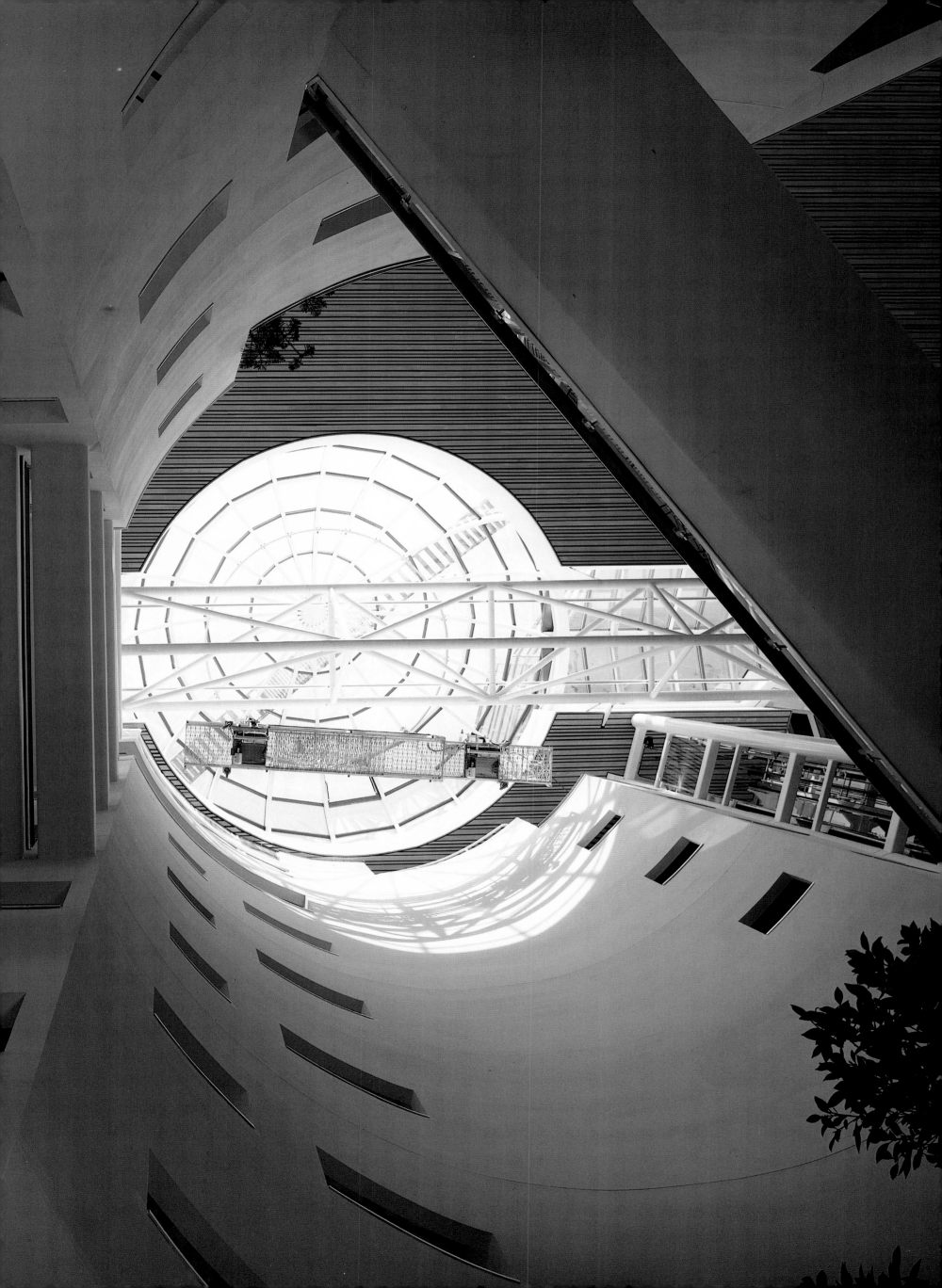

In contrast to the
conventional
speculative office
building The Ark is
more than skin deep;
it provides an interior
geometry that is
complex and enticing.
It can be experienced
in a number of ways –
both horizontally
and vertically – with
spaces that have
been created
expressly to make
places rather than
merely to respond
to function.

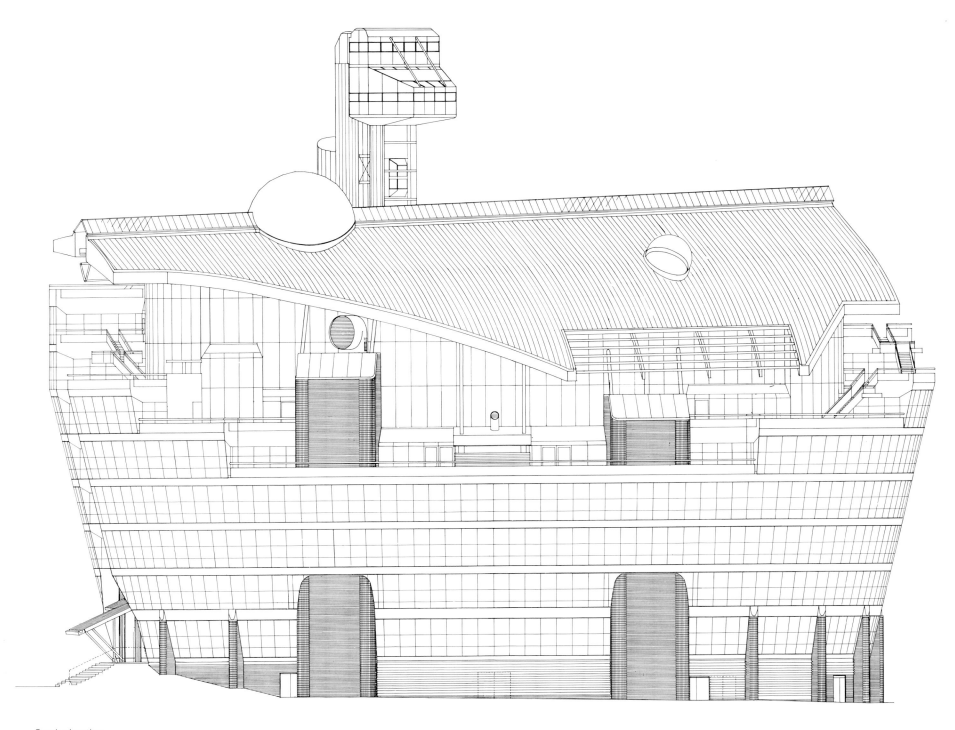

South elevation

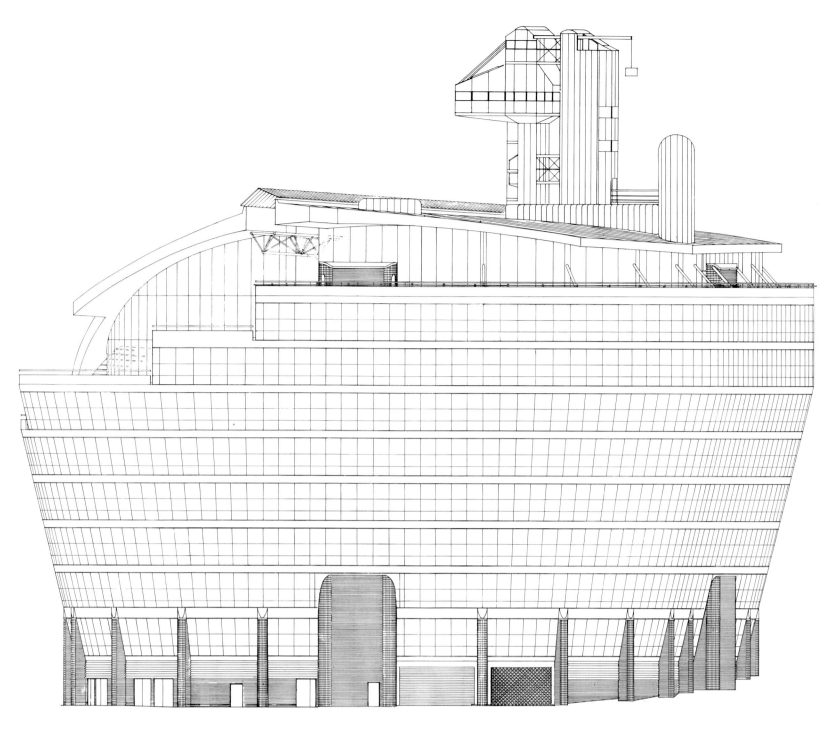

East elevation

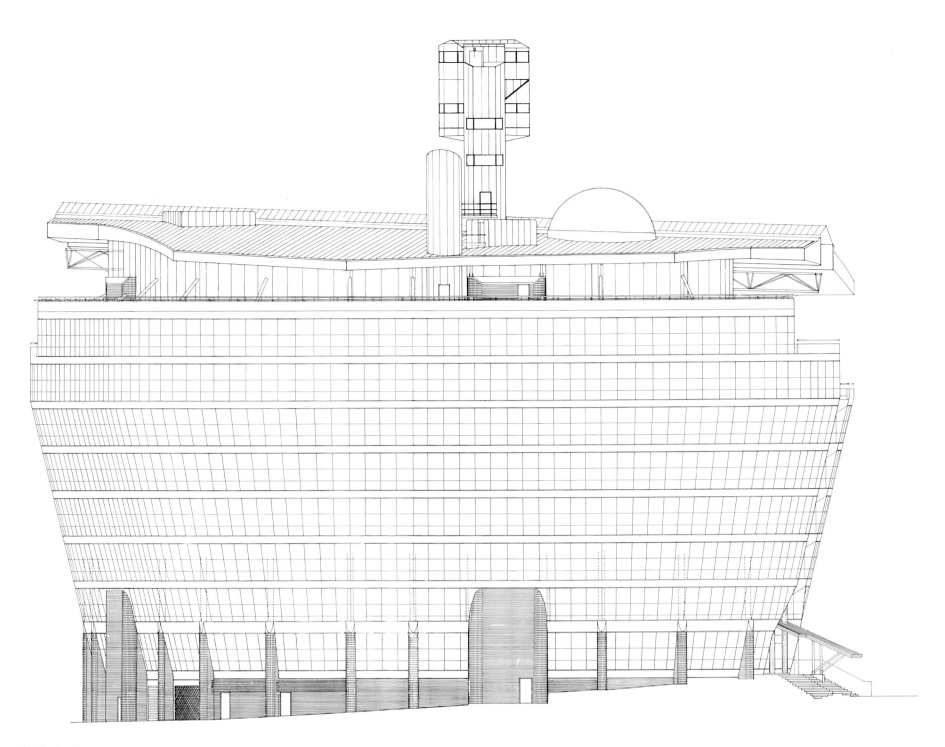

North elevation

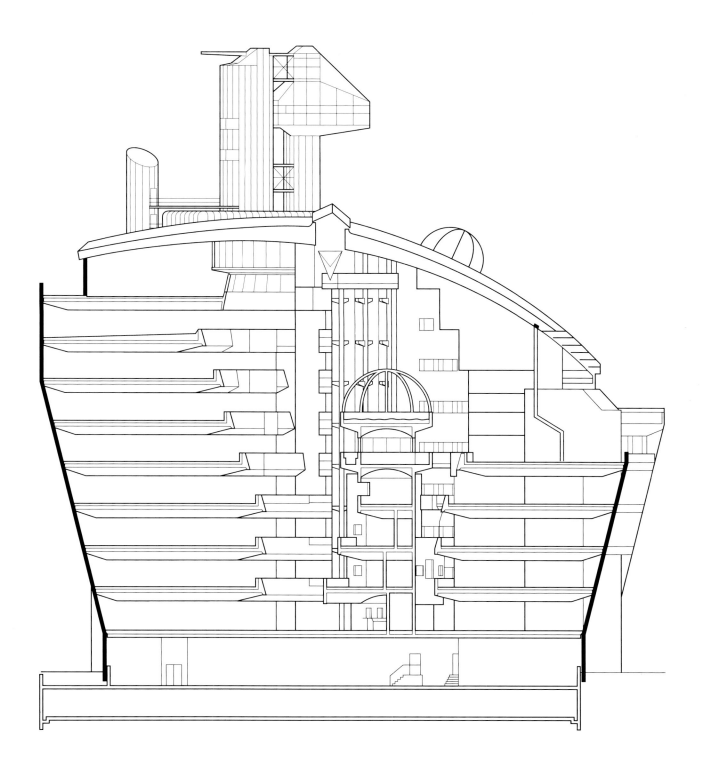

Section

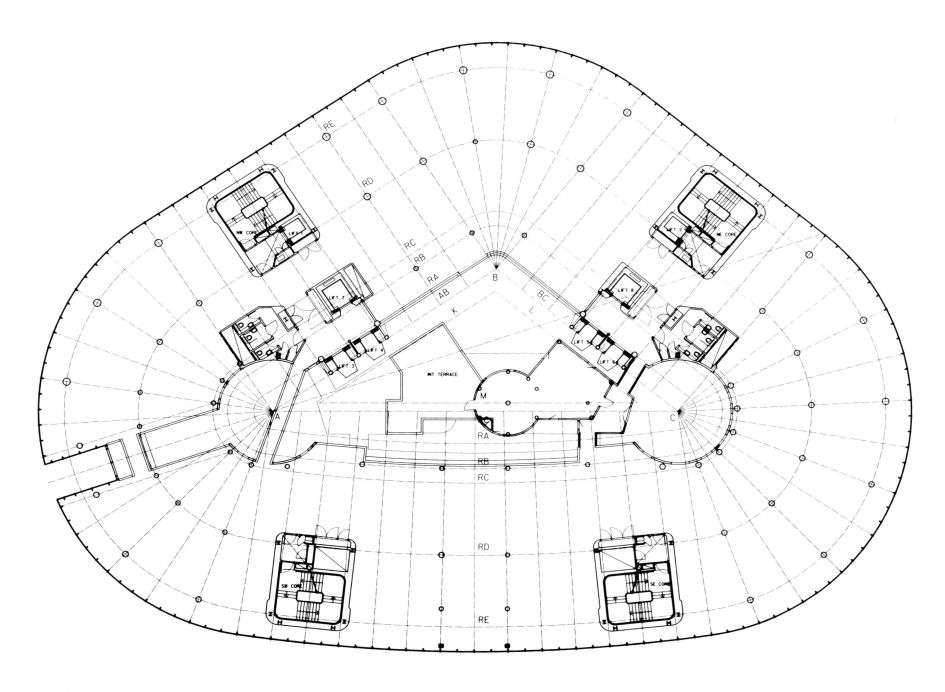

Level 4 plan

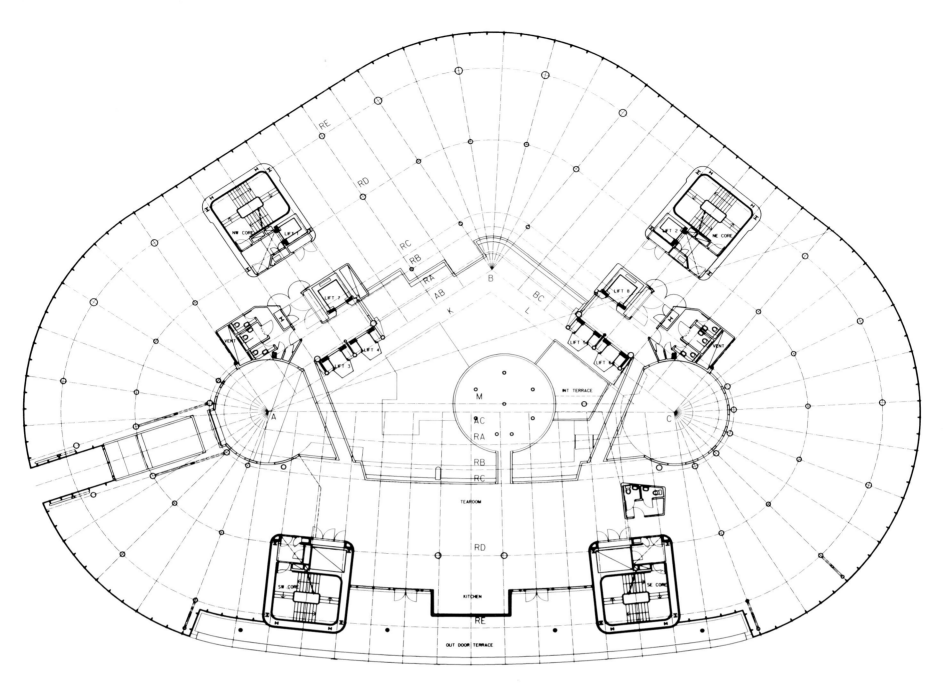

Level 5 plan

**Architects**
Ralph Erskine
Lennart Bergström
Arkitektkontor
Rock Townsend

*Project & Construction Manager*
Åke Larson Limited

*Structural Consultants*
Scandiaconsult AB
Andrews Kent &
Stone

*Mechanical Consultants*
Scandiaconsult AB
Dale & Goldfinger

*Electrical Consultants*
Gösta Sjölander AB
Dale & Goldfinger

*Acoustical Consultants*
Scandiaconsult AB
Arup Acoustics

*Fire Consultant*
Arup Research &
Development

*Landscape Architect*
Jakobsen Landscape
Architects

*Lighting Consultant*
Lighting Design
Partnership

**Ralph Erskine CV**

1932–1937
Studied architecture
at Regent Street
Polytechnic,
London W1

1941–1942
Own house, "The
Box", Lissma

1942–1943
Lida Leisure Centre,
Tullinge

1944–1945
Studied at School of
Architecture, College
of Art, Stockholm

1947–1948
Nilsson House,
Gästrikland

1947–1948
Mattress Factory,
Köping

1947
Avasjö Chapel,
Borgafjäll

1948
Ski Hotel,
Borgafjäll, Avasjö

1950–1953
Cardboard Factory,
Fors, Avesta

1951
Housing,
Jädraås,
Gästrikland

1953
Pulp Factory,
Hammarby,
Gästrikland

1954
Tesdorpf House,
Skövde

1954
Shopping Centre,
Luleå

1954
Rented Apartments,
Lassaskog, Växjö

1955
Engström House,
Lisö Island

1955
Office & warehouse,
Stockholm

1957
Arctic Town

1960
Bakery & offices,
Malmö

1961
Ortdrivaren Housing
Area, Kiruna

1962–1968
Barberaren Housing
Area, Sandviken

1963
Housing, Svappavaara

1963
The Erskines' House,
Drottningholm

1968
Clare Hall,
Cambridge (UK)

1968
Killingworth,
Newcastle (UK)

1969
Studlands Park,
Newmarket (UK)

1968–1982
Byker, Newcastle (UK)

1972
Bodafors Church,
Småland

1973–1978
Nya Bruket, Sandviken

1973
Easlestone, Milton
Keynes (UK)

1974–1981
University Sports Hall,
Frescati, Stockholm

1977
Vallhov, Sandviken

1977–1986
Myrstuguberget,
Huddinge

1978–1981
Tapetseraren,
Sandviken

1979–1983
Östra Steninge,
Märsta

1981–1986
Malminkartano,
Helsinki (Finland)

1983–1989
Ekerö Centre,
Tappström

1984
Vasa Terminal
Stockholm

1986
Ice skating rink,
Märsta

1986
Office premises,
Göteborg

1986-1990
Housing, Umeå

1986
Hospital dining room,
Stockholm

1987-1989
Housing, Ekerö

1987
Mixed development,
Stavanger (Norway)

1988-1992
The Ark, London (UK)

1990
Housing development,
Stenungsund

1992
CrossRail Stations,
London (UK)

1993
University Hall,
Frescati, Stockholm

All locations are in
Sweden unless
indicated.

**Blueprint Extra 10**

First published in
Great Britain in 1993
by Wordsearch Ltd
26 Cramer Street
London W1M 3HE
Telephone
071 486 7419
Facsimile
071 486 1451

ISBN 1-874235-10-4
Copyright © 1993
Wordsearch

*Distribution*
Faye Greenwell

*Design*
Patrick Myles

*Editing*
Caroline Roux

*Production*
Elena Acciarri

*Origination*
DawkinsColour

*Printing*
Cambus Litho Limited

*Photography*
Alan Williams:
pages 1, 4-5, 6, 10, 11
(bottom), 12 (bottom), 13,
17, 18, 19, 20-21, 23, 26-
27, 28, 34-35, 37, 38, 39.
Chris Gascoigne:
pages 14, 24, 25, 30-31,
32, 33, 40.
Martin Charles:
pages 8, 11 (top), 12 (top).